EDITH WILSON

The WOMEN OF OUR TIME® Series

EDITH WILSON

THE WOMAN WHO RAN
THE UNITED STATES

BY JAMES CROSS GIBLIN

Illustrated by Michele Laporte

VIKING

Wilson

Special thanks to Deborah Brodie,
who encouraged me to write a biography

For Morrell Gipson, another spirited Southern woman.
—J.C.G.

VIKING
Published by the Penguin Group
Penguin Books USA Inc.,
375 Hudson Street, New York, New York 10014, U.S.A.
Penguin Books Ltd, 27 Wrights Lane, London W8 5TZ, England
Penguin Books Australia Ltd, Ringwood, Victoria, Australia
Penguin Books Canada Ltd, 10 Alcorn Avenue, Toronto, Canada M4V 3B2
Penguin Books (N.Z.) Ltd, 182–190 Wairau Road, Auckland 10, New Zealand
Penguin Books Ltd, Registered Offices: Harmonsworth, Middlesex, England
First published in 1992 by Viking Penguin, a division of Penguin Books USA Inc.

1   3   5   7   9   10   8   6   4   2

Text copyright © James Cross Giblin, 1992
Illustrations copyright © Michele Laporte, 1992
All rights reserved

Library of Congress Cataloging-in-Publication Data
Giblin, James.
Edith Wilson: the woman who ran the United States / by James
Cross Giblin ; illustrated by Michele Laporte.
p.   cm.   —   (Women of our time)
Summary: A biography of the First Lady who gave vital support to her husband,
President Woodrow Wilson, and to the nation during and after World War I.
ISBN 0-670-83005-4
1. Wilson, Edith Bolling Galt, 1872–1961—Juvenile literature. 2. Wilson,
Woodrow, 1856–1924—Juvenile literature. 3. Presidents—United States—
Wives—Biography—Juvenile literature. [1. Wilson, Edith Bolling Galt,
1872-1961. 2. First ladies.]   I. Laporte, Michele, ill.   II. Title.
III. Series. E767.1.G52   1992 793.91'3'092—dc 20 [B]
91-42265   CIP   AC

WOMEN OF OUR TIME ® is a registered trademark of Viking Penguin,
a division of Penguin Books USA Inc.
Printed in the U.S.A.   Set in Garamond #3

CONTENTS

1

No School
for Edith

"I hate a *can't!*" Grandmother Bolling often told seven-year-old Edith. "Anyone can do anything they try to."

Edith paid close attention to what her grandmother said. Next to her parents, Grandmother Bolling was the most important person in her life.

Born in 1872, Edith was the seventh of 11 children. She and her brothers and sisters grew up in a crowded old brick house in the small town of Wytheville, Virginia.

Her mother was always busy with household chores

and had little time to spend alone with Edith or her other children. But Grandmother Bolling had time. She lived with the family and Edith was her favorite.

A fall from a horse had crippled Grandmother Bolling when she was young. Now she found it difficult to move about. Edith slept in her room and waited on her at all hours.

The old woman rarely left the house. So Edith served as her eyes and ears, reporting on interesting things she'd seen and heard in the neighborhood. She also took care of her grandmother's collection of 26 canaries.

Sometimes Edith found a young bird lying dead on the floor of one of the cages. Then she and her older brother Will played doctor and minister. They would wrap the bird in a piece of cloth, put it in one of Grandmother Bolling's spool boxes, and bury it in the bird cemetery they had started in the back garden.

In return for Edith's help, Grandmother Bolling was her teacher. There were no public schools in Wytheville, and the Bollings could not afford to send all their children to private schools. Before the Civil War, the family had been wealthy. But when Edith was growing up, they sometimes had barely enough money to buy food.

"My grandmother taught me nearly everything I know," Edith wrote later. "From her I learned to read and write. The Bible she knew from cover to cover, and we read it together morning and night. She also taught me to knit, to sew, to embroider, and to crochet."

Edith's father, a lawyer, did his best to teach his daughter arithmetic. And often, in the evenings, Mr. Bolling would read aloud to the family from the works of Charles Dickens or William Shakespeare.

Mr. Bolling told his children with great pride that they were related to the Indian princess Pocahontas. Pocahontas had married an English settler, John Rolfe, and they had a son, Thomas. Thomas Rolfe in turn had a daughter, Jane, who married Colonel Robert Bolling. Over the next 200 years, there came a long line of Bollings. Edith was thrilled to learn that she was one of them.

When Edith was 15, she went to a regular school for the first time. She was eager to study music, so her father arranged for her to go to a girls' boarding school in Abingdon, Virginia. It was known for its excellent music department.

Life at the school was not easy, however. The headmaster starved his students almost to death, Edith said, and gave them no heat in their bedrooms or in the music rooms. Sometimes her fingers became so stiff with the cold that it hurt to strike the piano keys. But she worked hard and made progress in her studies.

Despite the poor food at the school, Edith grew taller. By the time she came home in June, she had reached her full height of five feet, nine inches. This, along with her gray eyes, thick dark hair, and ready smile, made Edith stand out. She began to attract boyfriends, who gave her gifts of flowers and candy. Sixteen-year-old Edith enjoyed their attentions but didn't take any of the young men seriously.

After a year at home, Edith went to another boarding school, this one in the large city of Richmond, Virginia. She was much happier there and looked forward to continuing her education. But her father had to put her three younger brothers through school, so Edith was forced to cut short her own schooling.

She didn't question this. In Edith's day, it was considered far more important for a son to receive a high-school and college education than for a daughter to get one. Instead, she went to Washington, D.C., to stay with her married sister, Gertrude.

While she was in Washington, Edith met Norman Galt. Norman's family owned Galt's, the oldest and best-known jewelry store in Washington. Norman helped to run the business. At 27, he was nine years older than Edith, who had just turned 18. That didn't stop him from falling in love with her.

Over the next five years, in Washington and Virginia, Norman saw Edith often and tried to win her love. He was kind to her mother and father, and they urged Edith to consider him seriously. At last, in 1896, she said "yes" to Norman. Soon they married and settled down in their own small house in Washington.

Was Edith in love with Norman? She never said whether she was or wasn't. She wrote only that she "liked him immensely." But, as a young woman without an education or career, she knew she was expected to marry. And she believed Norman would make a good husband.

Their marriage had to meet many tests in the next few years. In 1899, Norman's father died, leaving Norman in complete charge of the Galt store. Later that year, first Edith's beloved grandmother and then her father passed away in Virginia.

Edith wrote that she "throbbed with pain." She had adored her father, and she would never forget all she had learned from Grandmother Bolling. But she pulled herself together and helped to sell the house in Wytheville. Then she brought her mother and three younger brothers to Washington. Norman gave the boys jobs in his jewelry business.

The worst tests were still to come. In 1903, a son was born to Edith and Norman, but he lived for only three days. As if that weren't enough, the doctors told Edith that she could have no more children. This made her feel so sad that afterward she never said or wrote a single word about her son.

Then, in 1908, Norman himself died after a brief illness. Edith may never have been in love with him, but she had come to care for him deeply. Now he was gone, and she was the sole owner of Galt's. What would she do? She had no business training or experience.

"I was immediately faced with the decision whether to continue the business alone, take in a partner, or close it up for what I could get," Edith wrote. She spent sleepless nights trying to decide which would be best.

On the one hand, she felt a responsibility to the employees of Galt's, some of whom had been with the firm for 20 or 30 years. Also, she, her mother, her younger brothers, and an unmarried sister depended on the store for almost all their income.

She decided to continue the business herself. Then she asked the store's manager to teach her what she needed to know about it.

Edith was a quick learner. Soon she was going over the store's accounts on a regular basis. She was also helping to make important decisions about its future.

Once she had the situation at Galt's under control, Edith relaxed and began to enjoy life again. She bought an electrically powered automobile that she delighted in driving around Washington. It was fun to pass a slow-moving horse and carriage and feel the breeze blowing through the veils on her hat.

Heads often turned when Edith drove by. There were few cars on the city's streets in 1910, and even fewer women drivers. Edith was the first woman in Washington to own an electric automobile.

Every year, Edith traveled to Europe, accompanied by her sister Bertha or a woman friend. She was in Paris in the fall of 1912 when Woodrow Wilson was elected to his first term as president, but she paid little attention to the event. She had never taken part in Washington politics and had never been inside the White House.

In the summer of 1914, with talk of war in Europe, Edith decided to vacation in Maine. She didn't want to be in France or Italy if fighting started there.

Edith's companion in Maine was a young friend, Altrude Gordon. Altrude was going out with the White House physician, Dr. Cary Grayson. Edith knew and liked the young man, and she and Altrude expected a visit from him during the summer. But Dr. Grayson couldn't get away from the White House.

He was treating President Wilson's wife, Ellen, who lay seriously ill. She died in August, at almost the same time the dreaded European war began. Now

the grief-stricken president was under more stress than ever. Dr. Grayson knew he must stay and look after him.

That fall, the doctor called on Edith in Washington. He had a favor to ask. He wondered if he might introduce Edith to the president's cousin, Miss Helen Bones, who was staying at the White House. She had been very lonely since the death of Mrs. Wilson.

Edith agreed to the idea, and she and Helen Bones began to go for hikes in Rock Creek Park. On these hikes, Helen told Edith many things about her cousin Woodrow. She spoke of his intelligence and the strength of his personality. She also told Edith how bravely he had carried on his duties as president despite his sorrow over the death of his wife.

Edith's imagination was fired by the picture Helen gave her of Wilson. But, she wrote later, "I felt he was too remote for me ever to have an opportunity to know him myself."

It wasn't long, however, before Edith did get a chance to meet Woodrow Wilson. And it came about as a result of one of her walks with Helen Bones.

2

Love and War

One afternoon in March 1915, Helen Bones picked up Edith in a White House car to go to Rock Creek Park. It was muddy in the park that day, and after their walk, the women's shoes were dirty. Helen insisted that Edith come back with her for tea at the White House.

"Oh, I couldn't do that," said Edith. "My shoes are a sight, and I should be taken for a tramp."

Helen explained that President Wilson was playing golf that afternoon with Dr. Grayson. There was no one at the White House to see Edith or her muddy shoes.

At last Edith agreed to go. But when she and Helen got off the elevator on the second floor, they immediately ran into the president and Dr. Grayson. The men had returned earlier than planned from their golf game. Edith chuckled when she saw that their shoes were even muddier than hers and Helen's.

After that chance meeting, a friendship quickly developed between Edith and Woodrow Wilson. In the next few weeks, she was invited to dinners at the White House, and the president began to go on afternoon automobile rides with her and Helen Bones. Edith met the president's three grown daughters: Nell and Jessie, who were both married, and Margaret, who was studying to be a singer.

The lonely president responded warmly to Edith's beauty, charm, and intelligence. She, in turn, was impressed by the handsome, well-spoken Wilson. He had been the president of Princeton University and the governor of New Jersey before he was elected president of the United States.

Edith was 42 when she met Wilson, and he was 58. But the president had the energy and drive of a much younger man. When he read poetry aloud to his White House guests after dinner, his compelling voice reminded Edith of her late father's.

Friendship soon turned into romance. Following a White House dinner in early May, less than two

months after they had met, Woodrow told Edith he loved her and wanted to marry her.

She was stunned. "Oh, you can't love me, for you don't really know me," she said. "And it is less than a year since your wife died."

But the president's love for her was real, and Edith continued to see him throughout the summer of 1915. When they weren't together, they exchanged letters almost daily. The telephone was still quite a new invention, and most people put their thoughts and feelings on paper instead of speaking them over the phone.

From the time they met, Wilson took Edith into his confidence. He told her all the things he was most concerned about as president. Among these were the latest developments in the European war.

England, France, Russia, and later Italy made up the group of nations known as the Allies. They had been battling the Central Powers—Germany and Austria-Hungary—for almost a year now. The Allies were fighting to defend their economic interests and to keep the Central Powers from conquering all of western and southern Europe.

The United States was neutral, meaning it had not taken either side and was not involved in the fighting. But President Wilson's sympathies, like those of many Americans, were with the Allies.

In May 1915, German submarines torpedoed and sank the British luxury liner *Lusitania*. Many of the passengers lost their lives, among them 128 Americans. President Wilson wrote a note of protest to Germany and showed it to Edith. She suggested that he make it even stronger, so he rewrote it and showed it to her again.

This time Edith approved of the note. Later, she wrote to Wilson: "Much as I enjoy your delicious love letters, I believe I enjoy even more the ones in which you tell me what you are working on—the things that fill your thoughts and demand your best effort. For then I feel I am *sharing* your work and being taken into partnership, as it were."

Edith had a hot temper, and sometimes it showed in her letters to Woodrow. Secretary of State William Jennings Bryan had resigned because he disagreed with the president's stand on the *Lusitania*. When Edith heard about this, she was furious.

"My blood boils when I think of that traitor," she wrote to Wilson. "I am afraid if he were left in my hands, I would put him where the world would never be troubled by him or his 'peace' sheep's clothing again!"

"How you can *hate!*" Wilson wrote back. "Whew! Isn't it rather risky to use mere paper when you commit such heat to writing?"

Woodrow and Edith weren't always so serious. They went to baseball games and took trips with friends and family on the presidential yacht.

Wilson discovered that Edith's favorite flower was the orchid. After that, he sent her a fresh one every day. "You are the only woman I know who can wear an orchid," he wrote on a card. "On everybody else the orchid wears the woman."

By September, Edith knew she was as much in love with Woodrow Wilson as he was with her. When he proposed marriage again, she accepted. The newspapers announced their engagement in early October.

Gifts came to the couple from all over the country. The people of California sent a large nugget of gold from the oldest gold mine in the state. Woodrow had part of it made into a wedding band for Edith.

They were married on December 18, 1915, in a ceremony at Edith's home. Only about 50 guests were present, all of them members of her family and Wilson's.

The president wore a cutaway coat and gray striped trousers. Edith, who was known for her sense of style, wore a black velvet dress and a matching black hat. A spray of white orchids and a large diamond pin brightened her outfit. Both were gifts from the groom.

In 1916, Wilson ran for reelection as president. Edith was by his side throughout the campaign. When he spoke to a gathering of native American voters in Omaha, she was introduced as a great-great-granddaughter of Pocahontas. The audience gave her a big round of applause.

Wilson was a Democrat and his Republican opponent was Charles Evans Hughes. The election proved to be very close. Although Wilson had kept the country out of war, many voters were afraid he wouldn't continue to do so. It wasn't until the last ballots were counted in California that the Wilsons knew he had won.

Edith had not been able to cast a ballot in the election. American women, led by a group called the suffragettes, had been seeking the right to vote for years. But they wouldn't get it until four years later in 1920.

Edith did not seem bothered by the delay. She had never been a suffragette and disliked their noisy ways. She was especially upset when they marched around the White House, demanding that the president support their cause.

With the election behind him, Wilson once more urged the nations of Europe to stop fighting. But his appeals had no effect. Instead, Germany stepped up its submarine attacks on both Allied and neutral ships, including ships from the United States.

"The shadow of war is stretching its dark length over our country," Edith wrote in her diary. She had begun the diary after moving to the White House.

At last President Wilson realized that all his efforts to keep America out of the war had failed. On April 2, 1917, he asked Congress to declare war on Germany. "The world must be made safe for democracy," he said.

Edith listened to her husband's message from the gallery of the Capitol. Afterward the Wilsons rode back to the White House through cheering crowds, but they themselves were silent. "The step had been taken," Edith wrote, "and we were both overwhelmed."

America quickly prepared for war and raised an army of four million men. Edith put to use the skills Grandmother Bolling had taught her. She joined a Red Cross sewing group that made pajamas for the Army. She also knitted warm wool caps for the soldiers who would be fighting in France that fall and winter.

Everything possible was being done to free manpower for the war effort. So Edith decided to get a small herd of sheep to graze on the White House lawn. The sheep would keep the grass cut while the gardener went to work in a war plant.

It wasn't long before the sheep began to multiply. When shearing time came, the original eight and their lambs furnished 98 pounds of wool! Edith sent it to

the Red Cross, which decided to hold a nationwide auction of the "White House wool" to raise money for the war. The auction brought in the amazing sum of almost $100,000.

During the war, President Wilson trusted Edith with all the secrets of his office. She learned a private code known only to Wilson and one of his closest advisors. Often working late into the night, she helped the president send secret messages to foreign countries and decode messages that came in from them.

In January 1918, Wilson made his famous "Fourteen Points" speech to Congress. The speech listed the goals for which America and the other peace-loving nations were fighting. They included freedom of the seas, firm limits on armies and weapons, and the founding of a League of Nations. The League would make sure that no country ever again threatened the territory or independence of another.

Edith read the speech in advance and was thrilled by the president's words. Everyone who heard the speech, she believed, would surely agree with its aims.

By the early fall of 1918, the war began to go in favor of the Allies. Austria-Hungary surrendered to Italy. Then the combined forces of the United States, Great Britain, and France launched a powerful new attack against the German army. The German defenses crumbled and the army retreated. On October 7, word reached Washington that Germany was asking for an immediate halt in the fighting. The Germans said they were ready to sign a truce, or armistice.

At 3:00 A.M. on November 11, a cablegram brought the president the long-awaited news that the Armistice had been signed. "The guns were still!" Edith wrote in her diary. "The World War was ended!"

She, along with all Americans, felt a tremendous sense of relief. But there was sadness, too. More than 53,000 American soldiers had been killed in the war, 234,000 had been wounded, and 4,500 were missing.

Now came plans for a meeting in Paris, France, to discuss the peace terms. President Wilson believed that his idea for a League of Nations should be linked to the peace treaty. He thought perhaps he should go to Paris to speak for the League in person.

Wilson's advisors urged him not to go. They reminded him that no president had ever left the country while in office. Edith, on the other hand, argued that he must go. She knew how hard it would be for the president to stay in Washington while the other Allied leaders were seated around the conference table in Paris.

In the end, Wilson agreed with Edith. On December 4, 1918, the Wilsons sailed for France aboard the liner *George Washington*. There was no possibility of their flying. This was more than 20 years before the first transatlantic passenger flights took place.

Edith relaxed during the voyage. The war that had darkened all their lives was finally over. Now she looked forward to years of peace and happiness with Woodrow.

3

Peace in Paris

When the Wilsons arrived in Paris, they were given a grand parade. Flowers rained down on Edith, bands played, and the crowd cheered, "Long live Wilson, the man who brought us peace! Long live America!"

The Wilsons settled into the palace that was to be their home in Paris. Soon afterward they went to visit the city's American hospital, where wounded American soldiers were being cared for.

Edith almost fainted. "I felt so ashamed," she said. "There they were, some with their entire noses blown away, some totally blind, others with chins and half

their faces gone. Well, I revived and stayed on and talked and told them how proud I was just to touch their hands."

The Wilsons got back to the palace in the early afternoon but did not want lunch. "Our hearts were too sad," said Edith.

On January 18, 1919, the peace conference opened in Paris. President Wilson rose to speak. He said the first order of business should be to draft a constitution for the League of Nations.

The leaders of Great Britain and France disagreed. They wanted to draft the peace treaty first and decide how much Germany should pay for the destruction caused by the war. However, Wilson took such a strong stand that he won over the other leaders to his point of view.

Edith attended none of the working sessions of the conference, but each evening Wilson filled her in on what had happened during the day. On her own, she visited schools and hospitals in Paris and an unheated gun factory where women had worked long, cold hours during the war.

"My hat goes off," Edith wrote, "whenever I think of these and other women whose names will never be on any honor roll."

One weekend during the conference, the Wilsons toured the city of Rheims, which had been heavily bombed by the Germans. The bomb damage, along with the wounded soldiers she had visited in hospitals, brought home to Edith the horrors of war in a way no book or picture could.

On February 14, the delegates to the peace conference voted to make the League of Nations a part of the peace treaty. Wilson was overjoyed. "A living thing is born," he said to Edith. That very evening the Wilsons left Paris for a brief trip to America.

When they got home, Woodrow and Edith were delighted to learn that many Americans supported the idea of a League of Nations. But 38 powerful Re-

publican senators were strongly opposed to the League. Their spokesman was Senator Henry Cabot Lodge, chairman of the Senate Foreign Relations Committee.

Lodge and the other senators feared that American soldiers would have to help defend foreign countries if the United States joined the League. They demanded changes in the League's constitution to make sure this would not happen.

Knowing he faced a hard fight, Wilson returned to Paris with Edith. There the president tried to get the Allies to accept the changes the Senate wanted.

Despite Edith's pleas that he take time to relax, Wilson worked day and night. He kept on working even after he was laid low with a severe case of the flu.

At last, in late April, both the League of Nations' constitution and the peace treaty were formally adopted by the Allies. Now the papers would have to be accepted and signed by Germany.

On Memorial Day, the Wilsons went to an American military cemetery outside Paris. There, among the rows of white crosses, the president made a strong speech. The great gift that those buried in the cemetery had left behind, Wilson said, was the League of Nations. It would help to insure that there would never be another war.

"This is an age that looks forward, not backward," Wilson said. "An age that rejects the standard of selfishness that once governed the councils of nations and demands that it give way to a new order of things in which the only questions will be: Is it right? Is it just? Is it in the interest of mankind?"

"When the speech was finished, people were sobbing," Edith wrote. "For myself, I could not speak for the tears."

Germany finally agreed to sign the peace treaty although it felt the terms were too harsh. The historic ceremony took place on June 28 in the Hall of Mirrors in the Palace of Versailles (say, "ver-SIGH"). All the

delegates, including Wilson, were dressed formally in black frock coats and top hats. The president ordered a spray of orchids for Edith to wear with her long gray gown.

Soon after the ceremony, the Wilsons sailed for home in triumph. The president presented the Versailles Treaty to the Senate. "Dare we reject it and break the heart of the world?" he asked.

To his dismay, Henry Cabot Lodge and other Republican senators were still opposed to the League. They wanted almost 50 new changes in its constitution. Unless these were made, there was a good chance the Senate would reject the entire treaty.

Wilson refused to ask for further changes. He had signed his name to the treaty as president, he said, and given his word in the name of the American people. He could not take it back now.

Wilson decided there was only one thing to do. He must make a cross-country railroad tour, speak directly to the people, and win their support for the League.

Edith and Dr. Grayson both tried to get him not to take the trip. The late summer heat would be at its worst, they argued, and he was still not completely recovered from the flu that had hit him in Paris.

But Wilson felt the future peace of the world was at stake. "I must go," he said to Edith. And so, on

September 3, the *Presidential Special* left Washington's Union Station.

On board with Woodrow and Edith were Dr. Grayson, the president's assistants, eight Secret Service men, and more than 100 reporters. They would be traveling almost 10,000 miles across the United States and back.

4

The President Falls Ill

Heat, crowds, and the constant roar of train wheels. That's what Woodrow and Edith had to put up with as the *Presidential Special* traveled across the country at an average of 400 miles a day. They rarely spent more than half a day in any state, and slept aboard the train on most nights.

Just before the train pulled into a new city, local politicians would come on board. It was Edith's job to greet and talk with them, and let only a few in to see the president. Then he would get off the train and speak to the crowd at the station or in a downtown auditorium. After the talk, he would climb back on the train and it would speed along the tracks to the next stop.

Wilson always responded to the children in his audiences. He said: "Nothing brings a lump into my throat quicker than to see the children that are everywhere the first to crowd up to the train when it stops. For I know that, if by any chance we should not win this great fight, it would be their death warrant. They belong to the generation that would have to fight the next war. . . ."

In Billings, Montana, several boys ran after the train. One was waving a small American flag that he wanted to give to the president, and he handed it up to Edith.

The boy next to him didn't have a flag, but he wanted to give the president something, too. A Secret Service man leaned over and took the boy's offering. It was a dime. Moved, the president kept that dime in a special pocket of his change purse.

As the president journeyed westward, he and Edith could feel the crowds responding more and more warmly to his speeches. But his opponents weren't standing still. Republican senators followed Wilson along his route. They made speeches of their own attacking the League.

Wilson traveled on, but his strength was not

limitless. He had many sleepless nights and began to suffer from headaches. Edith and his doctor begged him to slow down, to rest, to take a few days off, but Wilson refused. He had to keep going, he said, or else Senator Lodge and his other opponents would say he was "a quitter."

After stops in San Francisco and Los Angeles, the presidential train headed east once more. But Wilson did not relax his schedule and the headaches grew worse.

When Wilson got up to begin a speech in Pueblo, Colorado, he stumbled over his words and was silent for a long moment. A reporter wrote that Edith looked terrified. But then the president went on.

That night, Wilson had a blinding headache. Edith sat up with him until he finally fell asleep. The next morning, Wilson managed to shave, saying he had to get ready for his next speech at Wichita, Kansas. But when he came out of his room, the left side of his face was drooping and he spoke with difficulty.

Dr. Grayson told Wilson firmly that he must rest, but the president said, "No, no, no! I must go on!"

It was then that Edith stepped in. "Whether you like it or not, Woodrow, you're too tired to go on," she said gently. "You must stop for a while."

She reached for a mirror and held it in front of her husband. Looking at himself, Wilson was forced to

35

accept the truth of her words. When the train reached Wichita, the president's secretary announced that he was unable to give a speech.

The *Presidential Special* sped back to Washington, 1700 miles away. Dr. Grayson told reporters that Wilson's condition was due to overwork. He said the president was not seriously ill and would soon recover.

That seemed to be true when the train arrived in Washington. The president got off smiling with Edith and was greeted by his daughter Margaret.

Three days later, on October 1, Wilson said he felt much better. That evening he and Edith watched a movie in the East Room of the White House. Afterward, Woodrow read aloud to Edith for a while from the Bible. His voice was as strong as she had ever heard it.

But the next morning, the president told Edith he had lost all feeling in his left hand. He asked her to help him to the bathroom. She did so, but he was in such great pain that she left him to call Dr. Grayson.

While she was at the phone, Edith heard a noise. Rushing back to Wilson's bathroom, she found him lying on the floor unconscious. When the doctor arrived and examined the president, he confirmed what Edith had already guessed. Wilson had suffered a stroke that had paralyzed the left side of his body. Fortunately, his brain had not been affected.

Dr. Grayson prescribed complete rest. He announced that the president was "a very sick man," but did not say that he had had a stroke.

Once the president was out of immediate danger, those close to him had to decide how to proceed. There were still almost 18 months left in Wilson's second term as president.

Edith asked the medical experts called by Dr. Grayson to be completely frank with her about her husband's chances. One of the experts, Dr. Dercum, told her there could be no recovery unless Wilson were freed from having to deal with problems.

"How can I protect him from problems when the country looks to the president as its leader?" asked Edith.

Dr. Dercum advised her to examine everything that required the president's attention and try to handle as many items as possible without involving him. "Always keep in mind," the doctor said, "that every time you take the president a new problem, you are turning a knife in an open wound."

"Then had he better not resign, let Vice-President Marshall succeed to the presidency, and he himself get the complete rest that is so vital to his life?" said Edith.

"No," Dr. Dercum replied, "not if you feel equal to what I have suggested." The doctor believed it would be bad for the country if the president resigned. He also feared it would weaken Wilson's determination to get well.

The doctor urged Edith to consider his suggestion seriously. "The president has the utmost confidence in you," he said. "Dr. Grayson tells me he has always discussed public affairs with you. So you will not come to them unprepared."

5

Who's In Charge at the White House?

Edith did not want Wilson to be forced into retirement with the League not approved and his other work unfinished. So she agreed to help him as president in every way she could.

From then on, no one except Wilson's doctors saw him without seeing Edith first. She studied carefully all the papers that were sent to him from Congress and the various government agencies. Those she felt he should know about she presented to him in a short form.

After the president had read her reports, Edith took

handwritten notes of his comments and decisions. She sent these back to the agencies.

Some members of the White House staff were upset that Edith had taken charge. Joseph Tumulty had been the president's secretary and chief assistant ever since Wilson was governor of New Jersey. Now he could no longer get in to see Wilson.

This made Tumulty mad, and he accused Edith of shutting him out. He hinted that she was hungry for power. Edith got angry, too, and told Tumulty she was only doing what her husband wished.

Dr. Grayson, on the other hand, supported Edith. One day he praised the accuracy of the reports she made to the president. Edith told him that she had been trained to take careful note of what she saw and heard by her crippled grandmother. Now she was making good use of that training.

The vice-president, Thomas R. Marshall of Indiana, was glad the president had not resigned. Marshall had never been close to Wilson and did not want the responsibility of being president. But Henry Cabot Lodge and the other senators and officials who opposed Wilson were not happy with the situation. They wondered who was really running the country in that fall of 1919.

Up till then, first ladies had almost always stayed in the background. They expressed no opinions and took no part in public life. Now Edith seemed to be changing the rules.

Lodge and the others decided that she must be exposed. In speeches and articles, they called her "The Iron Queen," "The Presidentress," and even "America's First Woman President."

Their sarcastic comments hurt Edith, but she said nothing about them at the time. Only later, in her autobiography, *My Memoir,* did she defend herself. "I, myself, never made a single decision regarding . . . public affairs," she wrote. "The only decision that was mine was what was important and what was not, and the *very* important decision of when to present matters to my husband."

The situation reached a climax in December 1919, when a crisis developed with Mexico. Lodge and other senators questioned whether the president was able to handle it. A group headed by Senator Albert Fall was appointed to visit Wilson and find out for themselves.

Edith and Dr. Grayson feared the president might not be up to the meeting. But they decided there was no way it could be avoided. They prepared the president carefully and opened the White House to reporters for the first time since his stroke. Edith led Fall and the other senators into the president's bedroom.

The president sat up in bed wearing a sweater. Edith had rolled up the bedclothes to conceal his useless left arm. He had been freshly shaved and was smiling.

As Senator Fall took his seat he said, "We have all been praying for you, Mr. President."

"Which way, Senator?" the president said with a chuckle.

Wilson and his guests began to discuss the Mexican problem. Edith took notes of everything that was said so there would be a complete and accurate record of the meeting.

As the conversation went on, Senator Fall and the others realized that the president was still very much in command. He obviously knew what was going on in Mexico. He could even make jokes about his health.

After the meeting, the waiting reporters crowded around Fall. The senator had to admit that the president was alert and mentally fit. Wilson, with the help of Edith and Dr. Grayson, had passed an important test. Never again did anyone question his right to remain in office.

Meanwhile, though, he had lost another battle. Despite a last-minute plea from Edith, Wilson refused to consider any compromise with Senator Lodge on the peace treaty and the League of Nations. And so, when the treaty came to a vote in the Senate, it was rejected.

Edith worried how Wilson would take this rejection, but he reacted positively. "All the more reason I must get well," he said, "so that I can try again to bring this country to a sense of its great opportunity—and greater responsibility."

And he did get better in the next few months. By the beginning of 1920, Wilson was able to sit up for a few hours each day and do more work. Edith was almost always at his side, going over official papers with him and making notes of what he said. He often slurred his words because of the stroke. But Edith seemed to understand him even when others could not.

Although he was unable to walk, Wilson began to get around the White House in a wheelchair. He and Edith went out for afternoon rides again, but he had to be lifted in and out of the car.

Wilson's eyesight started to fail, so Edith read the newspapers to him each morning. In the evenings, after dinner, she read aloud to him from books, as Wilson had often read aloud to her in the early days of their marriage—and as her father had read aloud to the family when Edith was a little girl.

The year 1920 was an election year. The Republicans nominated Warren G. Harding as their candidate for president. Wilson did not seek the Democratic nomination, but he hoped it might be offered to him. Even though he was still very weak, he wanted another chance to work for the League of Nations.

Edith did not oppose her husband's dream. However, she was secretly pleased when the Democrats nominated Governor James Cox of Ohio instead. She feared Wilson would die if he tried to run for president again.

Cox promised Wilson that he and his running mate, Franklin D. Roosevelt, would speak out strongly in favor of the League, and both of them did so. But the Democrats went down to defeat on Election Day. The voters wanted to put the pain of the war years behind them and return to the "normalcy" that the Republicans promised. Harding won in a landslide.

The election results depressed Woodrow and Edith. They were cheered, however, by the opening of the first session of the League of Nations in Geneva, Switzerland, on November 15. And their spirits were raised even higher when news came in December that President Woodrow Wilson had been awarded the Nobel Peace Prize for his part in the founding of the League.

Now the Wilsons had to decide where they would live after they left the White House. They chose to stay in Washington. It had been Edith's home before her marriage. And Wilson could do research at the Library of Congress for the book about politics that he planned to write.

Every morning, Edith went out to look at houses in Washington. At last she found one that she liked. It was a comfortable, three-story town house with space for the president's thousands of books. There was also room to put in an elevator so that he could move easily from one floor to another.

One afternoon early in 1921, Edith entered Wilson's study at the White House and found him working at his typewriter. He pulled out the sheet of paper and showed it to her. It was the dedication for the book he intended to write after leaving the presidency.

Edith took the sheet and began to read:

"To Edith Bolling Wilson I dedicate this book because it is a book in which I have tried to interpret life, the life of a nation, and she has shown me the full meaning of life. Her heart is not only true but wise; her thoughts are not only free but touched with vision; she teaches and guides by being what she is. . . ."

6

Devoted to the End

Edith and Woodrow moved into their new home in March 1921, but Wilson never wrote more than the dedication to his book. He found it too difficult to concentrate. However, with Edith's help, he dictated an article on the world situation that was published in *Atlantic* magazine.

The Wilsons lived a quiet life, taking automobile rides in the afternoon and watching movies in the evening on a pull-down screen in the library. On holidays they entertained Woodrow's daughters and their families, and members of Edith's large family.

When the Wilsons went to the theater on Saturday night, the audience often applauded the former president. Edith was glad. The applause showed that people still loved and respected Woodrow, in spite of all the defeats he had suffered.

On November 11, 1923, friends arranged for Wilson to make a short radio broadcast to the nation from his library. It was Armistice Day, now called Veterans Day.

Wilson insisted on standing to read his speech into the microphone, saying he spoke better when on his feet. Even so, his voice sometimes stopped. At those moments, alert listeners could hear Edith prompting him from behind.

After the talk was over, Wilson felt it had gone badly. But the next morning, Edith read him the newspaper article that said his message had reached the largest radio audience up to that time—three million people.

By the beginning of 1924, even Edith had to accept the fact that Wilson was sinking rapidly. He lost consciousness and died on Sunday morning, February 3. At the moment of death, his daughter Margaret was holding his left hand and Edith his right.

When Edith heard that Henry Cabot Lodge was one of those named by the Senate to attend Wilson's funeral, she wrote a firm note asking him *not* to come.

She still had a hot temper. And she could not forget the pain Lodge had caused her husband during the fight over the League of Nations.

The funeral was held at Washington's National Cathedral. Hundreds of invited guests crowded into the chapel for the service. Thousands of other people stood in the rain and snow outside.

Edith placed a spray of black orchids on top of Woodrow's coffin. After the service, she watched as the coffin was slowly lowered into the cellar of the Cathedral, where it would be buried.

Edith stayed in Washington after her husband's death and devoted much of her time and energy to keeping his memory alive. She provided letters and papers to authors who wrote biographies of Woodrow. She also helped to restore his boyhood home in Staunton, Virginia, and make it into a museum.

After a Democrat, Franklin D. Roosevelt, was elected president in 1932, Edith was often invited to White House social events. On December 8, 1941, President Roosevelt himself invited Edith to sit in the gallery with his wife, Eleanor, when he asked Congress to declare war on Japan.

As she listened to the president, Edith couldn't help but remember her husband's speech in the same chamber in 1917, when he had asked Congress to

declare war on Germany. Within weeks, she was busy sewing for the Red Cross, as she had during the First World War.

After peace finally came in 1945, the United Nations took the place of the League of Nations. The United States played an active role in the new organization. Edith felt proud when tribute was paid to Woodrow Wilson during the founding ceremonies for the United Nations.

As the years passed, Edith's health began to fail, but her spirit was as strong as ever. She supported John F. Kennedy for the presidency in 1960. And she was invited to ride in the parade on the day he took office in January, 1961.

Although it was very cold, and she was a frail old woman of 88, Edith insisted on riding in an open car. It reminded her of the cars she and Woodrow had ridden in during the grand parades in Europe after the First World War.

On December 28, 1961, there was to be a dedication of the new Woodrow Wilson Bridge over the Potomac River in Washington. Despite icy weather and her own ill health, Edith was determined to attend. But during the early morning hours of December 28 she slipped peacefully into death. It was the 105th anniversary of Woodrow Wilson's birth.

Did Edith Wilson actually serve as president in those months when her husband lay partly paralyzed? No one will ever know for sure. There are no records of their conversations, except for the notes Edith took. But certainly she played a major role in keeping him and his presidency alive.

Edith Wilson never sought the spotlight for herself. As she often said, she was not a political person. She never promoted any social causes while she was first lady. Her only ambition, in good times and bad, was to help her husband.

Today, a president's wife probably could not play the role that Edith did. The 25th Amendment to the U.S. Constitution would prevent it. This amendment says that the vice-president shall immediately become the acting president if the president is unable to perform his duties.

However, a future candidate for president could learn much from Edith Wilson. In the difficult period after her husband fell ill, she showed a remarkable devotion, courage, intelligence, and sense of what was important. These are essential qualities for anyone— male or female—who hopes to be an effective president of the United States.

ABOUT THIS BOOK

On a trip to Washington, D.C., I discovered the warm, charming house where Woodrow and Edith Wilson lived after he left the presidency. It made me want to know more about the Wilsons, and led to the writing of this book.

Before her death, Edith willed the house and its contents to the National Trust for Historic Preservation. The trust maintains it as a memorial museum to Woodrow Wilson and his times. It is also a memorial to Edith. A portrait of her ancestor, Pocahontas, hangs on the wall in her bedroom. And her initials, E. B. W., can be seen on the needlepoint covers she embroidered for the dining room chairs.

Woodrow Wilson, with Edith always at his side, led the United States through the First World War and the struggle for peace that followed it. Many of the issues they had to deal with are still being debated today. That made this biography even more interesting to research and to write.

I didn't invent any of the dialogue in the book. It comes either from Edith Wilson's autobiography, *My Memoir,* or from the courtship letters of Edith and Woodrow.

J.C.G.